LifeCaps Press

Brontë

A Biography of the Literary Family

By Paul Brody

■BOŌKCAPS

BookCaps™ Study Guides

www.bookcaps.com

Table of Contents

About LifeCaps

LifeCaps is an imprint of BookCaps™ Study Guides. With each book, a lesser known or sometimes forgotten life is recapped. We publish a wide array of topics (from baseball and music to literature and philosophy), so check our growing catalogue regularly (**www.bookcaps.com**) to see our newest books.

Introduction

From humble beginnings, the Brontë family of Haworth, England reached a degree of literary fame that has seldom been replicated. Specifically, Charlotte, Emily and, to a lesser extent, Anne all made significant contributions to world literature.

The great tragedy of the Brontë family is that all were taken away by illness before the prime of their lives. Anne died aged 28 year; Emily died at age 30, and Charlotte lived the longest, dying in 1855 at age 38.

Each of the sisters struggled to make their way in a world that was not built with female independence in mind. Thus, they had do work for a living as teachers and governesses before finding success as authors. Even then, they kept their identities secret, knowing that female authors were simply not taken seriously.

Chapter 1: Origins of the Family

Born in Northern Ireland in 1777, Patrick Brontë had the unusual good fortune to rise out of his station in the world and move across the Irish Sea to England, building a respectable life for his eventual family. He was descended from a humble family of laborers, but at an early age the young man decided that he had higher ambitions. At 12, he was apprenticed to a blacksmith, but this scheme was short-lived. In his spare time, he taught himself to read, which distinguished him from his parents and family, and then taught others to read in small school when he was only 16 years old. He would even advance to the level of school principal before his accomplishments garnered outside attention. A local minister, the Reverend Tighe, took notice of the unusually bright young man, which set in motion a monumental change in young Brontë's life.

Tighe happened to be a Fellow of St. John's College in Cambridge. He sent Brontë to that illustrious school for a strictly religious, classical education. Brontë's goal was to become a member of the clergy, and he applied himself with extraordinary intensity. An Irishman at Cambridge was extremely unusual; he took immediate steps to distance himself from his undistinguished origins, only returning once to his homeland throughout the rest of his life. He altered his family name, Brunty, to Brontë, which he thought sounded more sophisticated. The name also sounded like the Greek word for "thunder," which revealed the Irishman's flair for drama. His lifelong habit of reading into the wee hours maintained his intellect and serious turn of mind but later contributed to his failing eyesight and near blindness.

Performing well at Cambridge, Brontë was soon granted his diploma, officially becoming the Reverend Brontë. His red hair, blue eyes and unusual height made him a favorite among the ladies, and at that point in life he was certainly interested in finding a companion. On December 29, 1812, he courted and married a woman from Cornwall, in the southwest of England, named Maria Branwell. Within a couple of years, they were celebrating the birth of their first child, Maria. After moving from one small community to another as the Reverend served out his duties as a curate, the family eventually settled in the northern town of Bradford in 1815 for what looked to be an extended stay.

In April 1820, the Reverend Brontë, together with his wife and children, left the town of Bradford and moved west to Haworth. All of the family's earthly belongings were hauled along difficult roads on seven carts. Brontë had accepted an offer to become the perpetual curate of the small community. There, he presided over the local congregation at St. Michael and All Angels Church. Located in the rugged and somewhat inhospitable Pennine Mountains, the area was continually cold, damp and cloudy, and many of the diseases typical of the time period were at epidemic proportions in the region. Because of an obsessive fear of fire, the Reverend forbade carpets and curtains inside the parsonage and kept buckets of water handy at all times. Haworth lacked anything like a sewer system, and the water was often contaminated. Owing to these conditions, the average age of death in the village was about 25. For various reasons, the Brontë household would always feel like outsiders in Haworth.

The reason for the move was purely economic. The Reverend knew that taking a position as the permanent spiritual leader of the community would give his family some stability; the family had the privilege of living in a (by their standards) spacious nine-room parsonage on top of a hill overlooking the village. Still, with so many children, plus hired help and a nurse for Mrs. Brontë, the five bedrooms quickly filled up. Surrounding the village and the parsonage was desolate moorland as far as the eye could see. This enormous natural playground would help to fire the imaginations of the Brontë children as they grew. The stern, distant nature of their father resulted in a relatively large amount of freedom for the children.

Six children comprised the Brontë family at the time of the move to Haworth. Maria was the oldest at six years old. She helped to care for the younger ones as her mother was quite ill. Elizabeth was a year younger. Charlotte had been born on April 21, 1816. Patrick Branwell, known by everyone as Branwell, was the only son—he was three at the time. Emily Jane was born on July 30, 1818. The last of the brood, Anne, was born on January 17, just three months before the family relocated.

The birth of her last daughter had left Maria Branwell Brontë seriously ill, with no sign of getting better. It's likely that she suffered from advanced stomach cancer given her symptoms. Her sister, Elizabeth Branwell, came to nurse Maria in her sickness. The children were mostly kept apart from their mother as she wasted away. On September 15, 1821, she finally succumbed to her long illness. Her last words were, "Oh God, my poor children." She was laid to rest in the Haworth churchyard.

Never really comfortable with his own children, the Reverend was not at all happy as a widower. But his strong desire for a new wife was not entirely selfish; he was thinking mostly of the care of his offspring and the maintenance of the household. He proposed to three successive women after the passing of Maria, and each one turned him down. However, his sister-in-law remained at the parsonage, helping manage the daily affairs as well as raise the children.

Aunt Branwell was an able caregiver and surrogate mother to the Brontë children, despite the fact that she didn't especially relate to children, being a "spinster" herself. The girls likely sensed this and, therefore, grew up without a strong mother figure in their lives. Emily would later make her Aunt an object of mockery, poking fun at her strict Methodism and lack of imagination; the hired kitchen servant Tabitha Ackroyd became more of a mother figure for Emily. Nancy and Sarah Garrs, hired nurses for the Brontë children, also filled this role until they left the parsonage in 1824.

Though she loved all of her brother-in-law's children, Aunt Branwell's favorite was Anne, who like herself suffered from asthma and was majorly petite. Anne also excelled at music, becoming quite accomplished at piano and music reading. Charlotte, too, was small and delicate. She had poor eyesight from an early age, but this didn't stifle her already noticeable intellect. In fact, Charlotte decided in childhood that she would be a writer when she grew up, a conviction that never wavered despite the curve balls that life threw at her.

The Brontë children were forbidden from playing with the children in the village, so they had to become their own playmates. Their constant togetherness helped forge the bonds of affection that would remain strong throughout their short lifetimes. The Reverend felt that his own family was of a higher class than the townsfolk, who mostly labored in mills and factories. He could also see the unique talents each of his children possessed, though naturally he maintained the highest hopes for Branwell as his only son.

The Brontë children who survived to adulthood became distinctive individuals, despite their early bonds and shared experiences. Emily, taking after her mother's side of the family, was generally considered the most attractive, and she was the second tallest member of the household after the Reverend. Charlotte remembered that her sister was harsh and not interested in socializing. She also had a toughness to her—she once was bitten by a stray dog and cauterized the wound herself with a hot iron. Branwell was the spoiled child, and his ability to get whatever he wanted would be his eventual undoing. Anne was quiet and reserved even in her youth, piously trusting that God would sort everything out. Finally, Charlotte was the comparative rebel and the ambitious one, who always worked hard to achieve her goals, not allowing setbacks to ruin her mood. She was the motor behind their literary aspirations, and if not for that, the world would have forgotten them entirely.

Chapter 2: Education

As with most aspects of life in Victorian England, the education of boys and girls differed in the extreme. While Branwell was expected to study the classics in preparation for a "manly" career in law, medicine or the clergy, the girls only required enough "refinement" to make suitable wives. The girls, therefore, learned to sew, draw and play music, while the Reverend instructed Branwell in Latin and classical Greek. Outside of this early formal instruction, the Brontë children learned much from the world around them, in addition to some popular magazines of the day and their father's relatively large library.

Blackwood's Magazine was a favorite of the Brontës. Containing imaginative stories of mystery, adventure and life in the country, *Blackwood's* was highly inspirational. When not occupied with tedious lessons in the parsonage, the children roamed freely on the moors. Emily was especially fond of the unforgiving, windswept, but strangely beautiful landscape. All of the children learned the names of the local flora and fauna and the various bird calls that could be heard in and around the village.

A practical and stern man by nature, the Reverend Brontë was already giving thought to how his daughters would support themselves as adults. In the early 19th century, marriage was typically the only path toward social mobility enjoyed by women. However, the families of young women were also expected to contribute a dowry—a sum of money paid on her behalf to bless the newlyweds. Brontë knew that having no money for dowries meant that his daughters were at a disadvantage, and so a "Plan B" had to be available. For women, the only viable option outside of marriage was teaching or becoming a governess, both of which required slightly more than the typical female education of the time.

To that end, in 1824 the Reverend sent two of his daughters—Maria and Elizabeth—to the recently founded Clergy Daughters' School at Cowan Bridge. The school was established as a place for respectable but poor families to send girls to receive a well-rounded education (at a charitable fee), all in preparation for a teaching career. Many of these establishments were quite good, but some were houses of horror. Cowan Bridge, unfortunately, was the latter.

Shortly after Maria and Elizabeth's arrival at Cowan Bridge, Charlotte and Emily followed. The fees for all four girls absorbed a quarter of the Reverend's income, but the necessity of an education could not be ignored. Charlotte described the place as a nightmare of cruelty and suffering, and it made an impression on her that lasted the rest of her life. The headmaster of the school, the Reverend William Carus Wilson, was a sadist by today's standards. All the girls had their hair cut short, supposedly to preserve them from feelings of vanity. The old stone building was perpetually cold and damp. Rather than wholesome food, the students were served burned porridge and dry toast. On Sundays, all the girls marched two miles to Carus Wilson's service in Tunstall, regardless of the weather. Not surprisingly, illness rampaged through the halls and classrooms.

Maria was the first Brontë to become ill at the school; despite losing weight and barely having the energy to stand, she was punished for being late and dirty and made to stand in the center of a classroom in humiliation. She took the abuse without complaint, but Charlotte was raging on the inside. Maria finally succumbed to her illness after being sent home in February 1825. Branwell and Charlotte were both devastated by the loss, but the tragedy was not complete. A month after Maria was laid to rest, Elizabeth was also brought home, suffering from the same affliction. She died in June, having lived only ten years.

Both Maria and Elizabeth were struck down by one of the deadliest diseases of the period: tuberculosis. Those unlucky enough to contract the disease endured horrible coughing fits as their lung tissue was destroyed. The pulse raced while the body was unable to convert enough nutrients from food to survive. The body wasted away as if it were eating itself, which gave the disease its common name of "consumption." The disease was contagious as well, so the close quarters of a cold, damp school house were a perfect breeding ground for an epidemic. Although the death of children was not unusual in the early 19th century, it was still traumatic, and one following on the heels of another was nearly too much to comprehend.

Fearing for the welfare of his remaining daughters, the Reverend Brontë pulled Charlotte and Emily out of Cowan Bridge, probably saving their lives. Free from the Reverend Wilson's torture chamber, the girls continued their education at home. The Brontë library provided more than enough reading material on a wide range of topics to satisfy each child's intellectual curiosity. Naturally, they each enjoyed an ample survey of the classics, such as Milton's *Paradise Lost*, the plays of Shakespeare, and the more recent work of the Romantic poets (Wordsworth, Lord Byron, and George Gordon, among others).

The wild, energetic verse of the Romantic poets helped to heighten the appreciation for the natural world that the Brontë children already had, thanks to the raw beauty of the Haworth moors. Emily was especially close to the land, and she often walked far into the countryside alone. For his part, Branwell was drawn to the work of Lord Byron, seeing himself as one of the adventurous heroes of the epic and scandalous poems.

In 1826, the Reverend Brontë, returning from a journey, brought a gift of wooden toy soldiers for Branwell. Each of the children, though, claimed one for their own. They gave fanciful names to their soldiers and used them to enact fantastic and imaginative plays; Anne name hers "Waiting Boy." From this dramatic play time rose the legendary realms of Angria and Gondal, imagined worlds rich with their own histories, legends and politics. Charlotte wrote tiny books detailing the goings-on in the world of Angria. Emily and Anne feeling somewhat pushed around by the elder Charlotte and Branwell, "seceded" to create their own island nation of Gondal. Everyone collaborated on maps of the various realms and portraits of prominent characters. Each child composed stories and poems based on Angria and Gondal. Almost two centuries later, it's not impossible to precisely filter out who created what; it is safe to say that the Brontë's imaginative play was a group effort. This play become even more sophisticated as the children got older, and sometimes even in adulthood the siblings would revisit their youthful creations.

The inspiration for Angria and Gondal came from real-world locations such as the Isle of Guernsey and the frozen Arctic, only recently explored by daring English gentlemen like Lord Bentinck and Sir Henry Halford. The magazines and natural history books in the Brontë library also provided material for the children's imaginative adventures and romances.

The playtime and self-directed learning of youth had to come to an end eventually. In 1830, the Reverend became seriously ill. Believing that he was near death, he began thinking hard once more about how to prepare a future for his children, especially his daughters. At 14, Charlotte was the first to be sent back to school (not, of course, to Cowan Bridge). After some investigation into the nature of the curriculum and the administration, Charlotte set off for Roe Head School in January, 1831. The price of tuition would, in fact, have been too costly for the Brontës if not for the contribution of wealthy Mrs. Atkinson, a family friend from nearby Bradford.

Being 20 miles away from home, Charlotte was naturally terribly homesick at first. But it was obvious that Roe Head School was a much better and healthier place than the dungeon of Cowan Bridge. The school was managed by Miss Margaret Wooler and her four younger sisters. They taught classes in French, grammar and geography, alongside the expected lessons in dancing, music, poise and manners. Here, Charlotte satisfied her massive thirst for knowledge, a trait that set her apart from her sisters. As a girls' school, Roe Head's overriding mission was to turn simple country girls into eligible wives for gentlemen.

Charlotte mastered the curriculum in a mere 18 months. She arrived at the school very well read but also significantly lacking in certain areas. She also earned a silver medal, the highest possible honor, in manners and speech for every term. When not studying, she made friends with Ellen Nussey and Mary Taylor, who both turned out to be lifelong confidantes. Nussey and Taylor were unconventional individuals; otherwise they would not have been so easily accepted by the Brontë sisters, who were anything but ordinary.

Meanwhile, back at the parsonage, Emily and Anne became inseparable in their sister's absence. When Charlotte did return home for breaks, she tutored her younger sisters in everything she had learned. She understood that she was helping to prepare them for teaching, should they be unable to find husbands.

Emily and Anne both eventually studied at Roe Head, with varying success. Emily traveled to the school in late summer, 1835, but only managed to stay for three months. She missed the familiar sights and sounds of Haworth too intensely. Unbearably homesick, Emily made no friends, and the school environment made absolutely no impression on her; she did what was required of her, but she was obviously suffering. Anne took her spot, but she too cared remarkably little for the confinement and expectations of a formal school. While she performed admirably, she was far from happy. In 1837, Anne left Roe Head for good after battling through a serious illness.

Chapter 3: Careers

In the summer of 1835, about the same time Emily Brontë was preparing for a journey to Roe Head School, her sister Charlotte was anticipating the same journey. But she wasn't traveling as a student anymore. Instead, she was to become the first of her sisters to be gainfully employed. She had accepted a teaching position with Margaret Wooler at Roe Head.

Almost immediately, Charlotte realized that she had no love for teaching. The same problems that annoyed her as a student were carried over into the role of teacher, not to mention that new problems were introduced. Most distressingly, she was beginning to devote serious time and attention to writing, but this of course conflicted with her responsibilities to the students. In the end, Charlotte became depressed as a result of being obligated to the young girls in her care. Homesickness, too, was a problem, and she longed for the familiar parsonage and the freedom of the moors.

In December 1836, while home for a holiday break, Charlotte took her first tentative steps toward a literary career. She sent a collection of writings to the famous Victorian poet laureate Robert Southey. At the same time, Branwell sent some work to William Wordsworth. While Branwell, to his discouragement, never heard anything back, Charlotte received an upsetting note from Southey. He recommended that, as a woman, she should turn her mind away from literature and toward the domestic pursuits more "appropriate" to her role in society. Charlotte was hurt and angry, but she didn't let the poet laureate's words stop her—if anything, she redoubled her efforts.

Back at Roe Head School, life became more complicated during the subsequent term. Anne, who was still plucking away at her studies, came down with what seemed like a serious cold. Charlotte was adamant that her sister should leave the school and go home to recuperate; Miss Wooler, on the other hand, determined that the illness was not so serious and that Anne could get better without having to leave. The disagreement turned into an ugly spat, with Charlotte using harsh words on her employer. As a result, Anne did go home, never to return to Roe Head. Charlotte left too, presumably forever, but in time she would return to the school and try to mend fences.

Before the 1838 school year, Miss Wooler moved her school to Dewsbury Moor. She also invited Charlotte to come back to her teaching position after the winter holidays. Reluctantly agreeing, Charlotte set off for Miss Wooler's school once more, but the old sense of homesickness would not go away. Likewise, the work load at Dewsbury Moor was no different than it had been at Roe Head, so quiet time for personal work was almost out of the question.

In July 1838, Branwell made his first halting steps toward a career of his own. He opened a portrait studio in Bradford, having developed a real talent for illustration and portraiture. As a man, there was far less shame in Branwell working for his living, whereas ladies took a step down the social ladder if they were required to work. Plus, by pursuing a refined occupation like the arts, Branwell could almost pass himself off as a gentleman.

Meanwhile, Emily left home to take a teaching position at Law Hill, not far from Branwell's studio. The only Brontë left at home besides the Reverend was Anne. The unmarried sisters knew that, at 61, their father had lived a full life already and could die at any time. Charlotte and Emily showed urgency in pursuing their respective teaching careers, but still, that wasn't enough to overcome the loneliness and frustration of managing so many young girls while almost never having time to themselves.

At Miss Pratchett's Law Hill school, Emily worked almost every day from 6 am to 11 pm. She quickly discovered that, like her older sister Charlotte, she had no inclination toward teaching. If anything, she was even less suited for the work, once remarking that she liked the school dog better than her students. The only positive effect of her time at the school was that it gave her motivation to take her poetry more seriously; some of her best verses date to this period in her life. As the second term got underway, Emily's health went downhill, probably owing to the tremendous workload combined with homesickness and depression. She came back home around the time of Christmas break in 1838-39, knowing that she would never leave Haworth again. Instead, she was satisfied to be a helper for Aunt Branwell, keeping the parsonage in order for her aged father.

Charlotte was already in Haworth by the time Emily got there; she had left Miss Wooler's employment for good near the end of fall term in 1838. For a time, all three sisters and Branwell were reunited. They happily went back to their childhood fantasies of Gondal and Angria. Later, when Charlotte and Anne had once more left to take on new positions, Emily battled a nagging sense of inadequacy. Unlike Charlotte, she had no social circle in Haworth, still preferring the solitude of the moors. She overcame her sense of failure by redoubling her efforts to keep the parsonage running smoothly. For a time, life was comfortably quiet, which was as good as Emily could hope for.

Soon, however, family events came to a crisis once again. At 22 years old, Branwell came home from Bradford, having failed to make his portrait business succeed. Too much time at public houses and too little time practicing his craft were the main culprits behind his failure. Also, he had trouble focusing his energy on one thing at a time, burning up his energy trying to be a writer, musician and portrait maker all at once. His failure was a crushing blow, not only for himself but also for the Reverend Brontë. In the meantime, the sisters (excepting Emily) once more were faced with the unpleasant choice between marrying or returning to teaching.

In Charlotte's mind, neither choice was acceptable. If following her ambition meant poverty and spinsterhood, she was OK with that. It was a minor surprise, then, when the Reverend Henry Nussey sent her a lengthy marriage proposal by mail, having only met her once, briefly. The businesslike approach of the Reverend did not appeal to her passionate nature. She had no qualms about turning him down, explaining to Ellen Nussey that she would only say "yes" to a particular kind of person.

Petite Anne received no such proposals. Instead, she traveled to the vicinity of Mirfield to take a position as governess with the Ingham family. In Victorian England, the status of the governess was complex and contradictory. These women usually came from respectable but not necessarily wealthy families. Those that employed a governess were indicating their own lofty position on the social ladder. Women like Anne were shouldered with many responsibilities while also expected to be somewhat invisible. The treatment of governesses ranged from kind to abusive, and everything in between.

The Ingham family consisted of five children, though Anne was responsible for only the two oldest: Cunliffe and Mary. She quickly found that, like Charlotte and Emily, she did not relate at all to children. Her position was complicated by her lack of power. She was expected to enforce discipline, but then the parents undermined that power by always giving in to the whims of their children.

Charlotte also tested the waters of being a governess, but she discovered that it was no better than teaching. In May 1839, she went to work temporarily for the Sidgwick family. The parents were typical of the class that employed governesses in that they totally ignored her while heaping the equivalent of a 16-hour workday upon her. When Charlotte wasn't managing her two charges, she was completing sewing projects for Mrs. Sidgwick. Despite the long hours and exhaustion, she successfully brought some order to the household. However, the interference with her own work was still too much to bear and all but permanently set her against the idea of being a governess as a lifelong occupation. About the same time she left the Sidgwick's home, Charlotte received another marriage proposal. Irish clergyman David Bryce, who had met her while visiting Haworth, was looking for a companion. Again, Charlotte politely refused. Bryce died several months later anyway, so a marriage would have been a tragedy. By this point, she was fully resigned to a spinster's life.

While the sisters struggled to find meaningful employment, Branwell had his own self-inflicted struggles. He found a respectable job tutoring two boys in a neighboring town, but was let go after only two months. It's unclear what happened, but more than likely his alcoholism or loose morals resulted in his dismissal. It would not be the first time that he committed self-sabotage.

Back at the parsonage, a new presence in the village brought some excitement for Anne. William Weightman came to Haworth to be the Reverend Brontë's curate, or assistant. He was friendly and flirtatious with all of the Reverend's daughters but especially so with Anne. Everyone noticed: a marriage proposal was expected, but never came. With a heavy heart, Anne left the parsonage in 1840 to become a governess for the Robinson family in York. Weightman's philosophy of love conquering all did have a strong effect on Anne's literary output as it's evident to some degree in all of her lead characters.

As Anne left for York, Branwell, through a network of associates, got a position with the railway. It was not a terribly difficult job, and he was soon promoted to station account manager. All was going well until 1842, when it was discovered that his books didn't quite match up. There were several pounds missing. No one accused Branwell of theft, but it didn't matter. The railway couldn't afford to pay a salary to a seemingly incompetent account manager. Once more, he was fired from a decent job.

Charlotte, left in the lurch after her brief stay at the Sidgwick's home, found another governess position with the John White family. There, she tutored a girl and boy, and they behaved remarkably well. Even more importantly, the parents were especially nice to her, giving her all the time off she needed to visit friends and family. Still, the essential problem remained. Charlotte didn't like work, at least not the kind of work she had to do for other people. She poured out her thoughts in a diary, but felt powerless to get off the merry go-round of teaching and governessing.

During a holiday that brought all three Brontë sisters together, they concocted a plan to take charge of their lives. By opening their own school, they could apply their education to a noble purpose while not having to work under anyone else's thumb. Pamphlets were printed out, and word was spread of the new girls' school. Miss Wooler, retired from teaching, offered to let the sisters use the Dewsbury Moor property as their base of operations. Aunt Branwell contributed money to the venture. Everything seemed to line up in their favor, except for one thing: the location was not favorable. Haworth and the surrounding areas were perceived as wilderness, and respectable families saw no reason to send their daughters so far into the north of England, no matter how highly regarded the teaching staff. No pupils meant no money, so the ambitious plan never got off the ground. Secretly, Emily was not half as disappointed as Charlotte. She was never wholly behind the idea in the first place. Instead, Emily had become far more preoccupied with her own writing and ideas than either of her sisters.

The failure of the Brontë sisters' school was a setback for Charlotte, but she didn't let it stifle her for too long. A letter from her old friend Mary Taylor was the catalyst for an exciting adventure, but also some heartache and regret. Taylor was living in Brussels, studying with her Uncle Abraham at his school. The family was wealthy but unconventional and had a more modern perspective on female education. Taylor invited Charlotte to join her for a six-month term.

Aunt Branwell and the Reverend Brontë readily agreed to Charlotte's sabbatical. It was also decided that Emily would join her—it was much safer for two young ladies to travel together. Once in Brussels, the Brontë sisters discovered that the Taylors' school was more expensive than their budget allowed for, so they looked around the city for alternatives. They soon found that the Pensionnat Heger, a local girls' boarding school, would give them the opportunity to teach and study for which they traveled across the English Channel to experience.

Both Charlotte and Emily received a warm welcome from Monsieur and Madame Heger, despite their odd manners and awkward silences. Constantin Heger saw the talent of the Brontë sisters almost immediately, and he made it his special project to nurture the work of Charlotte. The Belgian students, though, were even less tolerable to the sisters than their English students had been.

Although he could be cold and irritable, Constantin Heger instilled lessons in Charlotte that would remain with her throughout her career as a creative writer. He stressed ideas like clarity and the search for the "perfect word" to express a feeling or idea. Emily, on the other hand, was less conducive to accepting criticism, even of the helpful variety. An astute educator, Heger saw that Emily needed to preserve her own voice and style, and so he gave her plenty of latitude.

Living in a city like Brussels was a drastic change from the familiar and humble confines of the parsonage at Haworth. The sisters' unfashionability was on display every time they left the Hegers' school. For her part, Emily cared not at all for fashion. She wore out-of-date and ill-fitting dresses while Charlotte at least made an attempt to fit in and be sociable. In conversation, though, the sisters stood out even more, mostly by their silence. Whereas Charlotte was obviously just shy, it seemed that Emily was aloof and detached. In her diary, she recorded that Brussels felt like a kind of exile from her beloved homeland. She made only one friend during her entire stay in Belgium. Louise de Bassompierre was much younger and came from a far different background, but she and Emily seemed to be kindred spirits.

In July 1842, Madame Heger, highly pleased with the presence of the odd but brilliant Brontë sisters, asked them to stay on another six months, to which they agreed. A few months later, a pair of tragedies darkened the mood. First, Martha Taylor, Mary's sister, died, then a letter came with news of William Weightman's passing. He likely died of cholera, a horrific tropical disease that caused sufferers to die from dehydration. Martha Taylor may have died from the same disease, which had made its way into England and Europe only recently. The sisters grieved for Anne, knowing that the curate's death would affect her deeply.

The bad news kept coming: As summer turned to fall, Charlotte and Emily had to rush back to Haworth as Aunt Branwell was near death from a blocked intestine. Travel was much slower then, and they only arrived in time for the funeral. Anne took leave from the Robinsons during her aunt's illness, so all three sisters were reunited for a short time, although the circumstances were unfortunate.

Aunt Branwell had saved money her whole life, with the anticipation of helping her nieces after she was gone. The Brontë sisters were like the daughters that she never had. Each was left with about 300 pounds—quite a lot of money in 1842, but not enough to forego the need to earn a living. She left nothing for Branwell, assuming that, as a man, he would have opportunities to make his own fortune in life. Of course, his alcoholism, opium addiction and depression impeded those opportunities more than once.

After the funeral and reading of the will, it was time once more to go their separate ways. Anne returned to the Robinsons at Thorp Green, taking her brother along with her. She had managed to get him a position tutoring young Edmund Robinson, Jr. Charlotte, meanwhile, was eager to get back to Belgium, while Emily was happy to stay at the parsonage. She understood that her Aunt Branwell had been an indispensable helper for the Reverend Brontë; she was ready and willing to step into that role and remain in Haworth forever.

Bucking convention, Charlotte traveled alone to the coast and boarded a ship for Belgium. Once back at the Hegers' school, she took over the English curriculum and continued taking private lessons from Monsieur Heger. The professional relationship was blossoming into something deeper, at least from Charlotte's perspective. Madame Heger was not blind; she saw that her young teacher was entranced by her husband and took steps to cool the relationship. She stopped inviting Charlotte into the family sitting room, and she forbade any more private lessons. Previously friendly, she became stony and distant. In fairness, it was unlikely that Constantin Heger returned any of Charlotte's feelings. He was attracted to intellect, but not in any romantic sense.

Stymied and isolated, Charlotte slipped back into a depression. On a particularly dismal day, she entered an inviting Catholic church and gave confession, despite being a lifelong Protestant. She decided before the fall term of 1843 that her time at the Hegers' school was nearly up and announced to her employers that she was leaving at the end of the year. They implored her to stay—she was an excellent instructor, despite what seemed like some personal foibles—but she was insistent. About the same time, Mary Taylor invited her to come to Germany and teach at a coed school, but she declined this offer, as well. Charlotte continued teaching through December, and then returned to Haworth, never again to return to Belgium.

For a time, Charlotte worked to keep her connection to Constantin Heger. She sent letters and sketches once or twice a week, unbeknownst to Madame Heger. When she found a letter from her former employee in a waste basket, she forbade her husband and Charlotte from communicating more than twice in a year. It was essentially the end of their association.

The "break up" with Monsieur Heger was difficult for Charlotte. She was always susceptible to depression and irritation, and her experiences in Belgium left her feeling depleted and lonely. As a way to focus her energies elsewhere, she reconsidered opening a school for girls. Rather than rent out a dedicated space, she imagined that Emily and herself could use the parsonage and its extra rooms. These could easily accommodate 5 or 6 students. But again, the difficulty of establishing a school in the region was that no one wanted to go all the way out to the "wilderness" of Haworth.

In June 1845, Anne came home unexpectedly from Thorpe Green, where she had been governess to the Robinsons for five years. Branwell, who was there to tutor young Edmund, followed shortly thereafter. Anne did not discuss the reason for their return, but it soon became an open secret. Branwell had started a love affair with Mrs. Lydia Robinson, his employer's wife. When Mr. Robinson found out, he was of course fired. Naturally, Anne could not stay in a position that was so awkward, and so left for home. Branwell's reputation was permanently scarred, although he didn't seem to care about such things. Instead of trying to make things right, he slid once more into a haze of alcohol, opium and depression.

Branwell's shame was an encouragement for Charlotte to get away from the parsonage, but her hope for a return of affections from Monsieur Heger kept her in suspense. Apparently, though, the effect of Madame Heger putting her foot down was enough to terminate any budding relationship. By November 1845, Charlotte had given up all hope. About this time, a letter from Mary Taylor arrived, requesting once more that Charlotte come to Germany, but she again refused.

Charlotte was becoming indispensable to her father's work: his many years of avid reading by candlelight had steadily dimmed his sight. He needed help preparing sermons and sometimes even walking, and Charlotte proved an able helper. Soon, a new curate arrived to shoulder some of the Reverend's burdens. Arthur Bell Nichols was less easygoing that the late William Weightman, but he was kind and inoffensive.

The Reverend Brontë's eye problems came to a head in August 1846. Accompanied by Charlotte, he traveled to Manchester for corrective surgery on his cataracts. The surgeon only performed the operation on one eye; in the event something went wrong, he wouldn't be totally blinded. The surgery was performed while the Reverend was wide awake, with no anesthesia. He wasn't the only one suffering. Charlotte was dealing with an excruciating toothache, though she didn't complain.

Recovery from the eye surgery was long and slow. For several weeks, Charlotte was her father's nurse and companion. Meanwhile, as the Reverend gradually improved, his son rapidly worsened. In December, the family had to scrape money together to save Branwell from being imprisoned for debt. He had developed the habit of charging his bills at public houses throughout the region, as well as extorting friends and family for any spare cash. The weather did little to lift anyone's spirits, the winter of 1846/47 being one of the harshest in anyone's memory. The entire parsonage fell ill at one time or another.

The last couple of years of Branwell's life were dismal. When he tried to pull himself out of his addiction, he suffered from withdrawal. By 1848, it was clear that his alcoholism was only part of his problems. He lost weight and developed the cough that was the sure sign of consumption, or tuberculosis. Drugs and alcohol may have eased his physical pain, but they sped his overall decline. On September 14, 1848, he died, after having made a deathbed conversion for his father's benefit; for the Brontë sisters, the untimely passing of their brother was mostly a relief. For years, he had been a monstrous burden on the family. They grieved for his lost potential, but were thankful that his long suffering was over.

The disease was not finished: before another year had passed, Charlotte laid her remaining two sisters to rest. Emily was the first to show signs of illness. At Branwell's funeral, she developed a cold chill that worsened, becoming a racking cough with shortness of breath. In typical fashion, she refused the attention of doctors and insisted on going on with her daily routine. She became irritable when Charlotte or anyone else made remarks about her declining health. Less than two months later, on December 18, she fell down while taking food to the family's dogs. She died the following afternoon, so wasted away that the carpenter remarked he had never made such a small coffin for an adult.

After a bleak Christmas, Anne became ill. A minor cough became steadily worse. Desperate to stall death, the Reverend Brontë brought in a specialist to see if Anne's health could be restored. Mr. Teale's prognosis, though, was not good. Charlotte was not kept in the loop of her sister's condition, but she could figure things out well enough on her own.

Sensing her own failing vitality, Anne expressed a wish to go the seashore at Scarborough. Mr. Teale approved, believing that the sea air might restore some of her energy. Victorians believed in the power of a change of scenery to heal the body. They did not yet understand, however, the danger of contagious diseases. On May 25, Charlotte and Ellen Nussey accompanied Anne to Scarborough, where she walked the boardwalk and mixed with healthy vacationers. She died on May 29 and was buried by the sea, the only Brontë sister not laid to rest in Haworth. In the space of 9 months, three of the four children who grew up together on the moors were gone. Only Charlotte was left to preserve their memories.

By any measure, 1849 was the most difficult year of Charlotte's adult life. Still, she managed to publish a second successful novel in the wake of *Jane Eyre*'s fame. At this point, Charlotte's carefully maintained veil of anonymity was beginning to fall away, much to her annoyance. After a package from her publisher was accidentally opened in Keighley, the rumor began circulating in that community as to Charlotte's second identity as Currer Bell. A brother of Mary Taylor spread the word in his community. At the same time, a former classmate at Cowan Bridge noticed too many similarities between that school and the fictional Lowood portrayed in *Jane Eyre*. She put two and two together and pegged Charlotte as the likely author. When the critic George Henry Lewes heard rumors that the novel's author was indeed a woman, he took the opportunity to reiterate his belief that women should be having children, not writing stories.

During the second of two trips to London at the invitation of her publisher, Charlotte struggled to stay out of the spotlight. At private parties, William Makepeace Thackeray insisted that he knew who she actually was; she became so annoyed with the famous novelist that she had to leave the room at least once. She much preferred the company of Harriet Martineau, although she was a confirmed atheist.

A trip to Scotland brought Charlotte into the company of Elizabeth Gaskell, who was to become her official biographer. Gaskell had established her own fame in literary circles as the author of *Mary Barton*. At picturesque Lake Windermere, she also made the acquaintance of Matthew Arnold, another poet laureate, though she didn't particularly like him at first.

It soon became obvious that Charlotte's publisher, George Smith, had romantic designs on her, despite being several years her junior. He invited her on a vacation tour of Germany's Rhine river; Ellen Nussey cautioned Charlotte about returning his kindness too enthusiastically. George's mother strongly opposed any match, knowing the Brontë family's long history of tuberculosis and early mortality. Still, Charlotte did join Smith in London to view the thousands of booths and other curiosities of the Great Exhibition of 1851.

Eventually, Charlotte could not ignore the fact that her publisher viewed her as more than a friend. She decided to put some distance between them before any awkwardness could spoil their business relationship. She declined two further invitations to London, choosing to busy herself at the parsonage instead. A renewal of grief occurred when Keeper, Emily's dog, passed away from old age. Whether because of this grief or otherwise, Charlotte became seriously ill in the winter of 1851/1852.

The first symptoms of illness were a loss of appetite and a pounding headache. These complaints ominously recalled the consumption that struck down Emily and Anne only a few years earlier. Then, Charlotte developed a severe pain in her side, and the doctor diagnosed her with a liver disease. He gave her mercury pills to take, which of course resulted in poisoning. Somehow, her body persevered through illness and bad medicine, and she had the energy to travel to Scarborough and visit Anne's grave. The fresh air helped revive her somewhat, and she was soon writing again at full steam.

In December 1852, Arthur Nicholls proposed to Charlotte. She was taken totally by surprise and asked if he would wait until the next day for her answer. The Reverence Brontë was furious—he couldn't believe that his curate had made such an offer without his approval. Charlotte didn't need her father telling her not to marry Nicholls, as she had already decided against it. She had another novel in her yet, and she rightly guessed that getting married would put an end to her life as she knew it.

Elizabeth Gaskell came to the parsonage in September 1853, mostly to hear Charlotte tell her life story and show her the important places of her youth. Gaskell understood immediately the effect that the windswept moors had on the development of the literary Brontë sisters.

In her native surroundings, Charlotte made quite an impression on Gaskell. In a short space of time, she had endured after the loss of her three adult siblings. She continued writing and did not pine for a love match that she knew could never be. But her health was beginning to fail. She suffered a stroke in early 1854. Arthur Nicholls, who had moved on to another district after Charlotte's refusal of marriage, came back to help at the parsonage. The always outspoken Tabby Ackroyd informed the Reverend Brontë that he was being selfish and coldhearted by denying his daughter a good match in Nicholls. She convinced him to relent, and Charlotte was engaged to the curate in March 1854.

June 29 was a pleasant day in Haworth, but especially so for Arthur and Charlotte, as it was their wedding day. The Reverend Brontë, Ellen Nussey, Miss Wooler, Tabby Ackroyd and Martha Brown were the only guests in attendance. The newlyweds spent their four-week honeymoon in Ireland. Upon their return to Haworth, Arthur took over the Reverend's duties.

As she predicted, Charlotte wrote no more novels after her marriage. In fact, marriage to Arthur had drawbacks that she could not have predicted. For instance, he at first insisted on reading all of his wife's letters, both those sent and received, in order to give his "approval" to the contents. Ellen Nussey protested vigorously. Nichols relented on the condition that she burn all of Charlotte's letters after reading them; she agreed, but did not follow through on the promise.

Longtime family servant Tabby Ackroyd passed away in February 1855 after having lived a remarkable 84 years. Charlotte became ill nearly the same time, and it was clear that she would not live many more days. Like her sisters and brother before her, she was struck down before the age of 40. She died on March 31, 1855, just 37 years old.

Chapter 4: Literary Productions

The four surviving Brontë children—Branwell, Charlotte, Emily and Anne—spent much of their childhood together composing epic and complex tales of imaginary kingdoms. Branwell and Charlotte took charge of the land of Angria, while Emily and Anne, feeling somewhat excluded, founded their own realm of Gondal. Many of these narratives and histories still exist, at least in partial manuscripts. The children's obsessive interest in these fictional places helped set the stage for more mature writings.

In the fall of 1845, Charlotte accidentally discovered some of Emily's poems in one of her two secret notebooks. Before that, she didn't even know that her sister was writing anything other than letters and journals. Charlotte was utterly taken by surprise; the poems were remarkable and powerful. Emily was not pleased at having the curtain pulled back on her private, creative self, and flew into a rage. She soon calmed enough to listen to the praise and constructive criticism offered by her sister.

Anne voluntarily revealed that she had been writing verse, too. Hers were more straightforwardly religious in nature, often evoking gloomy, morbid moods and ideas. The three Brontë sisters decided, mainly at the urging of Charlotte, to create a single volume containing all of their best work. In February 1846, *Poems* was sent to the publisher Aylott and Jones. The work contained 61 individual verses on nature, love, loss and faith. The sisters wisely decided to publish under male pseudonyms: Currer, Ellis and Acton Bell. This improved their odds of success significantly. Interestingly, none of the Brontë sisters revealed their authorship, not even to family or close friends. The sisters' inheritances from Aunt Branwell enabled the production of *Poems*; otherwise, their literary ambitions may never have come to fruition.

Poems earned some attention from a few critics, who offered generally positive reviews, but sales were dismal. The collection only sold two copies. The most notable aspect of *Poems* was that it sparked curiosity surrounding the identities of the Bell "brothers." Some already suspected that the names were pseudonyms. In light of the poor sales, though, Charlotte realized that to earn a living at writing, they would have to produce novels, as these sold far better than poetry collections. It was Charlotte's initiative and persuasiveness, as usual, that urged her sisters to each try their hand at writing a novel. What she didn't know was that they had already started down that path on their own.

Each of the Brontë sisters had been working on novels independently, but each kept their work a closely guarded secret. In July 1846, they sent three separate manuscripts to the first of many London publishers: *The Professor*, by Currer Bell; *Agnes Grey*, by Acton Bell; and *Wuthering Heights*, by Ellis Bell. A full year passed before a publishing house expressed even the slightest interest. T. C. Newby agreed to print *Agnes Grey* and *Wuthering Heights* for an upfront cost of 50 pounds. It was the first, though certainly not the last, success the sisters would experience.

Charlotte

Interestingly, in the Gondal sagas of her youth, Charlotte never took on the character of a woman, instead showing her tomboy side by preferring male characters. Similarly, her first full-length novel was told from a male perspective; it wasn't until *Jane Eyre* that she embraced a female point of view.

One of Charlotte's earliest finished works was a novella completed while at Roe Head. *The Green Dwarf* was written under the pen name "Wellesley." The text was not published until 2003. Drawing heavily upon the Angria sagas, the novella imagines a war between two semi-fictional African kingdoms. It's likely that she was heavily inspired at this point by the work of Walter Scott, who wrote *The Black Dwarf* fantasy.

For the most part, though, the endless responsibilities of teaching left precious little time for Charlotte to think and write. Still, she somehow found the energy to begin work on a novel. The novel was composed in fits and starts, and she kept it a secret from virtually everyone. Meanwhile, in February and March of 1839, Charlotte composed a short story that described the happenings of an ordinary schoolteacher, Elizabeth Hastings, who left her home in the moorlands to take a new position in the city. Invigorated by her new surroundings, Miss Hastings makes many new friends and is recognized for her personal brilliance. In a sense, this was a fantasy of Charlotte's, but one that would soon be brought down to reality. Her first experience as a governess let her know that social class perceptions stood in the way of normal, human relationships between employers and employees.

After leaving the home of the Sidgwicks in 1839, Charlotte sent an incomplete manuscript to Hartley Coleridge, son of famous Romantic poet Samuel Taylor Coleridge, for his appraisal. As with Southey, his response was not encouraging. He too focused on Charlotte's gender rather than her talents. But neither Southey nor Coleridge could effectively discourage her from continuing down the path she had envisioned since childhood.

Charlotte's experiences in Belgium, both good and bad, provided fodder for her first abortive attempt to writing a novel. *The Professor* did not see publication until 1857, two years after her death. Her widower, Arthur Bell Nicholls, oversaw the reviewing and editing of the manuscript. During Charlotte's lifetime, *The Professor* was rejected so many times by publishers that she ultimately gave up on the novel, working elements of its plot into later work, particularly *Villette*.

The narrative of *The Professor* is a first-person portrait of the life of William Crimsworth, from his early youth to his career as a college professor, along with his mistakes and adventures along the way. His uncle had suggested that he become a clergyman, but this path was not appealing to William. Instead, he went to work as a clerk for his wealthy brother Edward. However, Edward mistreats his brother, possibly jealous of his refinement and intelligence. Mr. Hunsden, a teacher at an all-boys boarding school, sees William's qualities and rescues him from under the thumb of the cruel Edward. Mr. Taylor, headmaster of the Taylor's school in Belgium, was the inspiration for Mr. Hunsden.

William's hard work earns him the attention of the school's headmaster, Mr. Pelet. His reputation even spreads beyond the boys school; Mlle. Reuter, headmistress of a local girls school, offers William an enticing position at the school, which he gladly accepts. Soon, he finds himself developing feelings for Mlle. Reuter. However, Mlle. Reuter has already promised herself to Mr. Pelet, and William is heartbroken. From that point forward, he stifles his feelings and maintains a professional distance from his employer. Mlle. Reuter senses the change and attempts to bring William back to her. She asks him to instruct one of the other teachers, Frances, in modern languages.

Frances shows enormous promise and intelligence. Naturally, William becomes attracted to his fellow teacher. Mlle. Reuter, against her own best judgment, also develops feelings for William, and, therefore, becomes jealous of his attention to Frances. She dismisses the teacher, hoping to keep William for herself. Caught in an unpleasant love tangle, William decides to leave the school in search of Frances. He finds her in a graveyard; the couple acknowledge their feelings for one another, while William secures a high-paying position at a college. Now financially independent, the newlyweds start a family, found their own school and settle comfortably in the English countryside.

The themes that run through *The Professor* would become the prototype for the rest of Charlotte's work. These included the problems associated with human love, the distinctions between social classes, as well as an unsettling degree of anti-Catholic rhetoric. In 19th century England, open dislike of Catholics and the Catholic religion was not unusual, even among the well-educated and sophisticated members of society.

In the fall of 1846, as she nursed her father back to health from his painful eye surgery, Charlotte began assembling the pieces of her next novel. Early on, she imagined a heroine who resembled herself in appearance and personality. It would not be long before she broke through and connected with a publisher who realized her genius.

Whereas T. C. Newby agreed to publish Emily and Anne's first novels, Charlotte was disappointed by rejection. Another publisher, Smith, Elder and Company, while also rejecting *The Professor*, sent word to "Currer" that they liked the work but were interested in something longer and more expansive. In response, she sent the already completed manuscript for *Jane Eyre*. George Smith, the young manager of the publishing house, reportedly stayed up all night reading the novel. In a show of how highly he thought of the work, he offered Charlotte 100 pounds for the rights to publish the novel, plus royalties. He informed the unknown author that domestic and international royalties could total 500 pounds or more. This was a remarkable sum of money, and proved to Charlotte that she could, in fact, make a living by writing. Still, she kept her authorship secret for the time being, even from her father.

On October 19, 1847, Smith, Elder and Company published *Jane Eyre: An Autobiography*. The novel was picked up the following year for publication in American by Harper & Brothers, an enormous achievement for any British author. A later edition was dedicated to William Makepeace Thackeray, one of the leading authors of the generation. Charlotte's second finished novel was the first by a Brontë sister to reach the public eye. The novel was noteworthy, then and now, for showing just how violent and depraved charity boarding schools could be; the Victorian Age saw the birth of the first serious reforms in the area of child labor and child welfare, and *Jane Eyre* was undeniably a part of that ideology. At the same time, Charlotte showed as well any author before or since the awkwardness of being a governess. The Victorians were also concerned, but often silent on, issues of social class, so the story of Jane's mistreatment by her employers struck a nerve with many readers.

Not surprisingly, Charlotte's life experiences heavily informed the contents of *Jane Eyre*. For example, her friend Ellen Nussey's home, "The Rydings," became a model for Edward Rochester's Thornfield Hall. Similarly, her three months spent at the home of the Sidgwick's proved critical in describing the lowly life of a governess. In one incident, the young John Sidgwick actually heaved a book at Charlotte. This may have been the source of a similar event in *Jane Eyre*, in which John Reed throws a Bible at the innocent, young Jane. The Sidgwick manor itself, known as Stone Gappe, perhaps offered a model for Gateshead, where Jane Eyre spent part of her unhappy childhood.

Structurally, *Jane Eyre* was one of the first novels to fit the category of "bildungsroman"—a German expression meaning "novel of development." The novel closely follows the thoughts, feelings and decisions of the title character, giving an unequalled glimpse into human psychology. This innovation would be a strong influence on later authors like James Joyce and Marcel Proust. Charlotte explored numerous things that struck a chord, for better or worse, with her Victorian readers. For example, *Jane Eyre* seriously criticizes the kind of superficial Christianity that is maintained only for appearances. Likewise, the novel makes it clear that for women, life in Victorian England presented few opportunities. Perhaps most powerfully of all, Charlotte expressed through Jane the struggle between finding personal happiness and fulfilling society's expectations. Ultimately, Jane reaches a compromise that works for her. Many readers, however, read *Jane Eyre* as an attack on everything contemporary society held dear.

Published in three volumes, a typical arrangement of the period, *Jane Eyre*'s 38 chapters trace the life of the title character through five distinct phases. The novel begins with Jane 10 years old, an unwilling ward of her Aunt Reed. Her parents had passed away from typhus several years earlier. In the Reed household at Gateshead, Jane suffers constant physical and mental abuse at the hands of her aunt and cousins. Her recently deceased Uncle Reed was kind to her, but his passing left her entirely alone. After seeing a disturbing vision of her uncle while locked in the "Red Room," a doctor recommends to Aunt Reed that Jane be sent away to a charity school.

Life improves only slightly for Jane at Lowood School, which was based on the real-life Cowan Bridge Clergy Daughters School of Charlotte's own childhood. At Lowood, the sadistic headmaster, the Reverend Mr. Brocklehurst, has peculiar ideas about how to bring up young girls with a proper understanding of Christian duty. He advocates physical punishment and deprivation, keeping the rooms of the school bitterly cold and serving only the tiniest rations to the students. The 80 students suffer through repeated epidemics, which thin their numbers considerably.

Jane does make friends at Lowood, despite the brutal conditions. Miss Temple, one of the instructors, sees Jane's potential and gives her extra attention. Helen Burns, a fellow student, was modeled after Charlotte's sisters who did not survive Cowan Bridge—Maria and Elizabeth. Burns uncomplainingly endures punishment and starvation, eventually dying of tuberculosis in Jane's arms. After six long years as a student at Lowood, Jane graduates to the position of instructor. In contrast to the real-world events at Cowan Bridge, the fictional Lowood is reformed, and Brocklehurst removed from his responsibilities after the school trustees discover his cruel practices.

Exhausted with teaching, Jane puts out advertisements for herself as a governess; she only receives one response. Alice Fairfax, housekeeper of Thornfield Hall, requests an interview with Jane to assess her qualifications as governess to Adele Varens, a French ward of Mr. Rochester, master of the house. She is perfectly suited to the work and gets along well with Adele. In time, she even befriends the fascinating Mr. Rochester, an unusual occurrence that was not typical in the relationships between governesses and their employers. However, strange things begin happening around the house—disturbing laughter, an unexplained fire—that throw an air of mystery over the novel's events.

Jane realizes that she is becoming more than a little attached to Mr. Rochester when his courtship with Blanche Ingram ignites a fire of jealousy. She tries to suppress these feelings, but the engagement between Ingram and Rochester only further upsets her. Rochester sees this and changes course, proposing to Jane instead—a fantastic departure from the normal matches expected in "society."

On their wedding day, the significance of the strange events of Thornfield Hall are realized. Two unexpected guests, a Mr. Mason and his lawyer, announce that Mr. Edward Rochester is already married to Mr. Mason's sister, Bertha. Rochester had married Bertha in the West Indies, but she then descended into madness and violence. He explains that he keeps her in the attic with a nurse to take care of her. Horrified, Jane leaves Thornfield, unable to overcome her revulsion at learning that she almost participated in a bigamous marriage.

Desperate and confused, Jane wanders the roads and countryside of England, using up the last of her savings while looking for gainful employment. In one of the novel's several belief-stretching coincidences, she ends up on the doorstep of her cousin St. John Rivers, starving and penniless. He provides her with a safe refuge, even securing her a teaching position at a local school. After a few months, Rivers proposes marriage to Jane. But he's not interested in his cousin in a romantic sense. Instead, he wants a partner and helpmate for his upcoming missionary trip to England. Jane gives the proposal a lot of consideration, but soon news arrives that her uncle, John Eyre, has passed away and left her a fortune of £20,000—more than a million dollars in today's money.

Another seemingly supernatural occurrence helps Jane make the decision as to what to do with her life now that she's independently wealthy. One evening, when the moors are dark and quiet, she hears Rochester's voice calling to her, almost as if in a dream. As quickly as possible, she packs up a few belongings and races back to Thornfield Hall, only to find it a burnt-out ruin. It seems that while she was gone, Bertha set fire to the house, killing herself and severely injuring Rochester. Upon reuniting, Jane says that she would gladly accept another marriage proposal from him despite his disabilities and sordid past. The couple are married and soon have a son together.

As a pure reading experience, *Jane Eyre* delighted nearly everyone—at least those whom it did not offend. *Vanity Fair* author William Makepeace Thackeray complained that he lost an entire day of work to reading the novel. The critical establishment was mostly enthusiastic, too, with just a few holdouts who worried that the subject matter was distasteful or unbelievable. Some readers perceived that the author was a woman and downgraded the novel on that account. The style of *Jane Eyre* deftly combined elements of Gothic fiction with traditional English characters, such as the Byronic hero epitomized by Mr. Rochester. The supposedly insane woman locked away in the attic was a powerful image, which has resonated in fiction even to the present day.

In spite of the enormous, unexpected success of *Jane Eyre*, Charlotte remained perfectly anonymous in the village of Haworth. She turned down offers from her publisher to come to London and mix with high society. Her sisters were in on the secret of course, and she also sent a copy of the novel to Mary Taylor. At Anne and Emily's insistence, Charlotte finally broke the news to her father. His reaction was lukewarm, not surprisingly. It was the first and last time that any of the Brontë sisters included their father in their literary successes.

The people and events of Charlotte's life populated the world of *Jane Eyre*. Lowood School was a remarkable facsimile of Cowan Bridge, a fact not lost on local residents. The sadistic Miss Andrews, who made Maria suffer until she was nearly dead, was reproduced in the form of Miss Scatcherd. Jane Eyre's young friend Helen Burns evokes the memory of Maria Brontë in the way she gracefully accepted her punishments and illness. As an adult, Jane Eyre became governess for the Lady Ingram, whose name is frightfully similar to Ingham, a family for whom Anne briefly served as governess. Thornfield Hall many have had a real-world counterpart in North Lees Hall, a stately Elizabethan manor house visited by Charlotte and Ellen Nussey in 1845. Elizabeth Gaskell, Charlotte's biographer, revealed many of these parallels in *The Life of Charlotte Brontë*, published in 1857.

In July 1848, Charlotte and Anne traveled to London to meet George Smith in person. He was still under the impression that Charlotte was "Currer Bell." The two unassuming women had some difficulty getting an appointment with the busy publisher. Once in his office, they were silent, and Smith had no idea what they wanted. Charlotte then handed him a letter in his own handwriting addressed to Currer Bell. Smith put two and two together, astonished that the author of *Jane Eyre* was a plain, petite and quiet woman. He insisted that they travel around London together, seeing all the sights and meeting all the best people, but Charlotte declined; she wished to not reveal herself to anyone else.

With the buzz surrounding *Jane Eyre* still at a fever pitch, Charlotte began work on a new novel. In October 1849, *Shirley* was published. The novel dealt directly with the many social problems facing nineteenth century England. The novel was also powerfully influential in an unexpected way. Before its release, the title character's name (Shirley Keeldar) was considered a masculine name. Afterwards, Shirley became much more common as a girl's name. Writing *Shirley* was likely one of the most difficult tasks in Charlotte's life, as its composition took place at the same time she lost her three living siblings to illness and death.

The setting of *Shirley* is the fictional parishes of Briarfield and Nunneley. The novel's events take place in the shadow of both the Napoleonic Wars and the War of 1812, when a struggling economy combined with the Industrial Revolution put many factory and mill employees out of work. Charlotte called upon English history in creating this realistic backdrop, as her father had been a firsthand witness to the Luddite uprisings against work-saving machines.

The lead character of Caroline Helstone was loosely based on Anne Brontë. Shirley, on the other hand, was how Charlotte imagined Emily might have turned out had she been born to a wealthy family and lived a complete life. The maiden name of Mrs. Pryor, Shirley's former governess, was Agnes Grey, a nod to Anne's first novel of the same name; the character's personality borrowed from Margaret Wooler of Roe Head school.

The basic plot of *Shirley* concerns mill owner Robert Moore, who is trying to balance business success against the wellbeing of his workers. Two foreign wars and their associated embargos have put a strain on commerce; at the same time, new machine introduce efficiency at the cost of people's jobs. Some of his former employees plot to destroy the machines or harm Robert.

Young Caroline Helstone comes to the Moore house (Fieldhead) to learn French from Robert's cosmopolitan sister, Hortense. Caroline is absolutely penniless, having been raised by her clergyman uncle. She believes that both of her parents died when she was very young. The Reverend Helstone objects to Caroline's plan to become a governess, preferring that she find a suitable husband and not enter the working world.

When Caroline meets Shirley, the independent-minded and confident heiress, she gets a new perspective on the world. In the meantime, Shirley and Robert Moore seem to be courting, which is painful for Caroline as she has developed feelings for the mill owner. The sense of unrequited love plunges Caroline into depression and then physical illness. Shirley's former governess, Mrs. Pryor, intervenes with some startling news—she is, in fact, Caroline's mother. This stunning news helps her to recover her wits and health.

Shirley informs Caroline that she has no plans to marry Robert Moore, but is instead fond of his younger brother Louis, an impoverished tutor. She realizes that their different social statuses will make a marriage awkward, but doesn't care. Robert, who had left England mysterious, returns and confesses to Caroline that he has feelings for her, as well. A double marriage is arranged, and all loose ends are tied up neatly.

Overall, Charlotte's second novel had less mystery and romance than *Jane Eyre*, although readers who had been shocked and disturbed by the first novel found much more to like in *Shirley*. Overall, though, the response to the novel was muted—a "sophomore slump" for Charlotte. Rather than the first-person approach, Charlotte adopted a third-person, all-knowing narrator, a more traditional approach to fiction. Her friends the Taylors once again provided fodder for the novel. Their aristocratic estate, known as the "Red House," inspired Shirley's "Briarmains." The general vicinity of Roe Head School, where Charlotte rounded out her education, served as the setting for the novel, with its flat terrain and emphasis on modern industry. The entire Taylor family, in fact, was transformed into the Yorkes, with Mary becoming Rose Yorke. Mary, not a dim bulb, picked up on the resemblances.

After an appropriate amount of time passed, during which Charlotte grieved for her lost siblings, she began work on what would become her last novel. *Villette* was published in 1853. Most reviewers heaped praise on the novel. Mary Ann Evans (George Eliot) considered it Charlotte's best work yet, better even than *Jane Eyre*. However, a cold and hurtful review from Harriet Martineau signaled the end of the friendship. Charlotte felt confused and betrayed.

Villette deals with the psychology of Lucy Snowe as she pursues a teaching career. Like *Jane Eyre*, the narration is in first person. The lead character may have been based on William Wordsworth's "Lucy" poems. Lucy hides many pertinent details from readers, and there are several supernatural occurrences, making *Villette* a distinctly Gothic novel. The fictional Kingdom of Labassecour, where Lucy eventually establishes her boarding school, is possibly modeled on Charlotte's juvenile Angria writings. The major themes of the novel essentially continue the author's tradition of questioning traditional gender roles, as well as the difficulty of conforming to a new culture. The ending of *Villette* is ambiguous; Lucy leaves readers to decide whether the conclusion is happy or otherwise.

Emily

Like her sisters and brother, Emily dove headfirst into creative writing, although she was significantly more secretive about what she was doing. She participated in the Gondal and Angria sagas, keeping the mythologies alive well into adulthood, when Charlotte and Anne had "grown out of" their juvenile writing phase. At some point, she began composing more personal and heartfelt poetry, dealing with heavier themes like love, loss, sin and homesickness.

Love poetry eventually became Emily's most powerful mode of expression, but her brand of love poetry was different from anything else being written. There was an intensity to it, and some literary historians have wondered if her love for her brother took on an unwholesome aspect. Many of her poems deal with a secret sin buried away in the past, and many have sexual overtones. Of course, it's impossible to make statements about an author's life based solely on their writing, but so little of Emily's letters and diary entries remain that the temptation to do so is extremely powerful.

As the Brontë sister who was at home in Haworth more so than Anne or Charlotte, Emily saw firsthand the steady, then sudden decline of Branwell into debauchery and near-madness. She was as disappointed as anyone, but her love for her brother did not waver. The emotional conflict was the fuel for much of Emily's creative endeavors.

In February 1844, Emily copied scores of poems written over the past several years into two notebooks. One notebook was dedicated to Gondal-themed poems; the other was for more intimate, personal work. The following year, Charlotte, while home on an extended leave, accidently happened across one of Emily's journals. But for this discovery—which sent her into a rage that did not cool for days—Emily might never have tried to publish anything that she had penned. Several days of cajoling from elder sister Charlotte were necessary before Emily relented and agreed to have 21 poems included in the sister's joint edition of *Poems*. Perhaps not surprisingly, she deliberately excluded her most intimate work, which just so happened to be her best. Even Charlotte recognized as she recorded in her diary, that Emily was likely the superior poet of the three.

Emily was forever burdened with the severe kind of self-doubt that is common among highly skilled but also extremely reserved creative artists. These doubts, coupled with her unfamiliarity with the world of publishing and business, meant that Charlotte took the reins, as usual. The themes and artistry behind Emily's first and only novel, however, were entirely of her own making.

As a child, Emily heard Tabby Ackroyd and other locals describe the heavy rain squalls that passed over the moors "wuthering." She never forgot the evocative word and planned to use it in her work later. From Tabby, she also learned ballads and stories that had been passed down through many generations of Yorkshire natives. The gloomy atmosphere of these stories no doubt had an influence on *Wuthering Heights*.

Owing to the lack of surviving diary entries and letters written by Emily, piecing together the story of her literary productions is more difficult than it is with her sisters. Evidence supports the theory that *Wuthering Heights* was begun during the period of Branwell's last decline into drug and alcohol addiction, possibly in the fall of 1845. Most of the novel was therefore written during the especially harsh winter of 1845/46; nearly the entire household battled severe cold and flu at one point or another, not to mention Branwell's drunken rages.

Thematically, *Wuthering Heights* deals with enormous and timeless issues through the lens of an ill-fated pair of lovers on the harsh moorland of northern England. The novel exposes humanity's most primal emotions, which resulted in a startled and frequently offended readership.

Most reviewers and biographers have noted the many way in which the characters of *Wuthering Heights* resemble people from Emily's own experience and even, in some cases, herself. Emily and Catherine Earnshawe's childhood, for instance, were both marked by physical and emotional isolation on the moors. However, both found enjoyment in this isolation, whereas many children would have felt deprived. Tabby Ackroyd, who had been almost a mother to Emily in her childhood, is reimagined as kitchen servant Nelly Dean, who like Tabby is fond of singing ballads while she works.

The novel's other main character, Heathcliff, shows a strong parallel to Branwell. They are both passionate but doomed, as well as being outcast from normal society. Heathcliff's love of the married Cathy mirrors Branwell's ill-conceived romance with Mrs. Robinson. In this sense, Cathy takes on attributes of Mrs. Robinson. Both suffered from fragile emotional states as their lives presented them with painful, difficult choices. At the same time, the love between Cathy and Heathcliff is inappropriate because he is, after all, a foster brother. This familial complication may have been based on Emily's too-intense love for her own brother.

Family and romantic love were not the only inspirations for Emily's singular masterpiece. Despite her repeatedly voiced distaste for traveling, her six months in Brussels may have given her one of the seeds for *Wuthering Heights*. It's there that she likely first encountered the writings of the German Romantic movement. Specifically, E. T. Hoffman's *The Entail* resembles Emily's later novel in terms of mood and form. Of course, being the socially isolated nature lover that she was, Emily put her own strongly individual stamp on the novel.

As was the case with her poems, Emily probably only published *Wuthering Heights* at the insistence of Charlotte, who was the "go-getter" of the three. For her part, Emily had no great ambitions of fame or fortune. Similarly, she had no social or business skill for dealing with the complex world of publishing and authorship.

Official publication of *Wuthering Heights* was delayed until December 1847. Emily made the mistake of keeping up a business relationship with the publisher T. C. Newby, who had established a reputation for dishonesty and swindling. His financial accounts were probably falsified, he delayed publishing the work of his authors, then delaying payment even longer, and finally he sent proofs to the press that were still full of typos. All things considered, the circumstances of the novel's publication nearly guaranteed its failure—or at least made success a difficult goal. For one thing, Newby hinted in the announcements for *Wuthering Heights* that it was, in fact, an earlier production of the author of *Jane Eyre*—essentially, that Currer and Ellis Bell were the same person. Naturally, both Emily and Charlotte were horrified. For better or worse, Emily's novel was compared to her sister's recent success, which served to diminish its impact.

Responses to *Wuthering Heights* broke into two camps. On the one hand, many readers and critics were simply confused. The novel was morbid, disturbing and rambling; there was simply nothing else like it at the time. Other were horrified by what they saw as inappropriate subject matter. *Wuthering Heights* revealed many of the darker aspects of humanity, things that the typical Victorian reader did not want to acknowledge. In her own defense, Emily simply wasn't worldly enough to realize that the fruit of her imagination would be so distasteful to a Victorian audience.

Wuthering Heights sold relatively well, though of course not nearly as well as *Jane Eyre*. The sordid subject matter likely kept many readers away while enticing others who secretly had a dark turn of mind. Sadly, it wasn't until a few years after Emily's death that critics slowly began to see the greatness of her only novel. Writing for *The Palladium Magazine* in 1850, Sydney Dobell was among the first to argue that Emily's work outshone that of either Charlotte or Anne.

A strange twist to the story of *Wuthering Heights'* growing renown was the claim made be friends of the late Branwell that he had been responsible for all or part of the novel. For a while, this theory held some sway over critics and biographers. However, the actual facts of the matter argue against such a possibility. For one thing, Branwell was simply too far gone with opium and alcohol to muster the energy to produce anything resembling *Wuthering Heights*. Eventually, this "conspiracy theory" lost traction, and today no one doubts the authorship of what has become the most celebrate novel produced by any of the Brontë sisters.

Wuthering Heights proved in time not only to be enormously influential but revered as one of the great novels in the English language. Some have wondered whether Emily might have gone on to create even greater work had she lived past 30. On the other hand, given that her experience of the world and its people was severely limited—she preferred being alone on the moors to anything else—it's uncertain that she could have had enough raw material with which to create another complete novel.

Anne

While laboring under the watchful eyes of the Robinsons at Thorp Green, Anne found the time to begin work on her first novel, *Agnes Grey*. It was the first completed prose work by any of the Brontë sisters, although it was published alongside *Wuthering Heights*. A second edition came out in 1850. The novel closely mirrors Anne's own life experience as she moved from one governess position to the next. Some of her employers were gracious, while others were cold and distant. Agnes ran into particular problems trying to discipline children, as the parents gave her no power but expected results anyway.

Agnes' first position as governess is in the Bloomfield household. There, the children rule the house tyrannically, and the parents always take their side. Young Tom Bloomfield actually tortures small animals, which allows the author to express a theme obviously important to her: animal rights. Mr. Bloomfield constantly sees something wrong with what Agnes does, and finally, after a year, she leaves.

Her next assignment is with the Murray family, where she finds the situation slightly better but not ideal. By this time, Agnes has let go of the idea that the rich are in some way superior to everyone else. The girls under her care—Matilda and Rosalie—are both spoiled. Rosalie is known as a flirt, and later she competes with Agnes for the attention of Mr. Edward Weston, the new clergyman. However, Rosalie marries Lord Ashby instead, who she does not love at all.

At the conclusion of the novel, Agnes and Mr. Weston are conveniently reunited, and he proposes marriages to the faithful and modest former governess. They have three children together and lead a happy, quiet life.

Agnes Grey garnered less attention than either *Wuthering Heights* or *Jane Eyre*. Reviews were mixed; few were overwhelmingly positive or negative. In recent years, the novel has received renewed attention and earned more praise than it did when originally published. Like Emily, Anne did not inform her father that she had published.

Anne did not disturb or surprise her readers, choosing to adopt a more conformist approach to literature. However, her work still contained subversive elements, although these were subtly expressed in comparison to her sisters' novels. For example, through the course of *Agnes Grey* it becomes clearer that the upper classes of society could be just as coarse and simple-minded as those born into poverty.

A visit from a Mrs. Collins, who lived in nearby Keighley, provided the foundation for Anne's second novel. She came seeking guidance as to how best to deal with her abusive and alcoholic husband. Rather unexpectedly, the Reverend Brontë suggested that she leave her husband. She followed through on that advice, building a respectable new life for herself and her two children.

Like many Victorian novels, *The Tenant of Wildfell Hall* was split into three volumes. The novel is structured in the form of a letter, otherwise known as an epistolary novel. The story begins with the arrival of Mrs. Helen Graham and her son Arthur to Wildfell Hall. The supposed widow becomes a source of intrigue and gossip in the community. She refuses a proposal of marriage from Gilbert Markham, instead giving him her diaries to read.

Graham's diaries recount her unhappy marriage to Arthur Huntingdon. Mr. Huntingdon holds wild parties for his friends at the family's home, Grassdale. All of these characters are portrayed as totally lacking in class and self-control, a depiction shocking to see for Victorian readers. Mr. Huntingdon even begins encouraging his son, Arthur Jr., to drink and use foul language. In some respects, *The Tenant of Wildfell Hall* is the most disturbing off the Brontë sisters' novels. Naturally, Helen cannot marry because she is already married—she fled Grassdale in secret, taking her son along with her. The novel was so edgy, in fact, that Charlotte stopped its republishing after Anne's death.

Helen travels back to Grassdale when she learns of her estranged husband's impending death. Even on his deathbed, Arthur does not see the error of his ways. Inheriting his fortune, Helen then moves into the estate at Staningley. Gilbert hears that Helen is now an eligible widow and goes to meet her. He his misgivings, though, knowing that she is now incredibly wealthy. However, Helen is able to look past their different situations, and the couple are soon married.

Female independence and the ravages of alcoholism were the main themes of *The Tenant of Wildfell Hall*. Anne had a better-than-usual understanding of both. She and her sisters formed a trio of female artists who had taken unconventional paths in life. Meanwhile, Branwell was suffering from delirium tremens, a symptom of withdrawal from alcohol.

The Tenant of Wildfell Hall was published through T. C. Newby again, despite his sloppy work with *Agnes Grey*. The publisher made the further blunder of telling a US publisher that "Currer" and "Acton" were the same person, thereby borrowing the success of *Jane Eyre* as a selling point for Anne's work. Naturally, this caused some confusion for George Smith, who had paid Charlotte for exclusive publication rights to her work. Sorting out this confusion was the motivation behind Charlotte and Anne's trip to London in July 1848. Emily was invited, but she declined; at liberty to go anywhere, she wanted to stay close to the parsonage.

Both *Agnes Grey* and *The Tenant of Wildfell Hall* dealt less with specific histories and regions and more with character types, such as the governess, the sinner, the invalid, the married woman, the mother and the artist. Each of these types were fairly recognizable to contemporary readers.

Anne had the misfortune of being measured against the work of her sisters. That line of thinking has persisted to the present day. In that sense, *Agnes Grey* is sometimes thought of as "Anne's *Jane Eyre*," and *The Tenant of Wildfell Hall* as her *Wuthering Heights*. Of course, those comparisons are unfair. For one thing, *Agnes Grey* was written before *Jane Eyre*, not to mention that each Brontë sister did indeed have a distinctive style. Recently, critics have made an effort to separate Anne's work from that of her sisters and give her the credit she deserves.

In general, Anne's work is an insightful exploration of secrecy and identity. For a woman in Victorian England, these were daily concerns. Whereas Emily ignored "society" and Charlotte found subtle way to subvert it, Anne looked for a compromise. She was an artist of her times, and her novels put a magnifying glass on the timeless struggle for self-realization.

Chapter 5: Legacy

As is often the case when noteworthy people pass away, friends and associates of Charlotte made efforts to preserve a certain image of the Brontë sisters. Many letters and other writings simply disappears. Elizabeth Gaskell, Charlotte's biography, framed her late friend's story in a particular way that appealed to Victorian readers. Charlotte herself had a powerful on influence on the image of the family and their collected works that was presented to posterity. In the wake of Anne and Emily's passing, she had sole control over publication of further editions of her sisters' novels and poetry. She revealed their identities in a new, three-volume edition of *Wuthering Heights* and *Agnes Grey*.

Several of the novels have been revived in the form of adaptations. *Jane Eyre* has been adapted into feature films, television programs and theatrical performances thousands of times, as has *Wuthering Heights*. In 1922, *Shirley* was adapted into a silent film.

As far as social impact is concerned, the effect of the Brontë sisters cannot be overstated. Feminist critics Sandra Gilbert and Susan Gubar titled their masterpiece on Victorian literature *Madwoman in the Attic*, a deliberate reference to the key plot point of *Jane Eyre*. Jean Rhyss' *Wide Sargasso Sea* tells the story of Bertha Mason from Bertha's perspective, calling into question the power relationships between colonizer and colonized, men and women. Meanwhile, Anne Brontë's *The Tenant of Wildfell Hall* has been widely recognized as one of the first entirely feminist works of fiction.

Today, the Brontë sisters are firmly positioned as among the most highly regarded novelists of their, or any, generation.

Bibliography

"Agnes Grey." (2013). Wikipedia.
http://en.wikipedia.org/wiki/Agnes_Grey

"Anne Brontë." (2013). Wikipedia.
http://en.wikipedia.org/wiki/Anne_Bront%C3%AB

"Brontë family." (2013). Wikipedia.
http://en.wikipedia.org/wiki/Bront%C3%AB_famil
y

"Charlotte Brontë." (2013). Wikipedia.
http://en.wikipedia.org/wiki/Charlotte_Bront%C3
%AB

Crandall, Norma. *Emily Brontë: A Psychological*
Portrait. Rindge, New Hampshire: Richard R.
Smith Publisher, Inc., 1957

Dimnet, Ernest. *The Brontë Sisters*. Trans. Louise Morgan Sill. New York: Harcourt, Brace and Company, 1910.

"Emily Brontë." (2013). Wikipedia. **http://en.wikipedia.org/wiki/Emily_Bront%C3%AB**

Frawley, Maria H. *Anne Brontë*. New York: Twayne Publishers, 1996.

Gaskell, Elizabeth. *The Life of Charlotte Brontë*. New York: Mershon, n.d.

Gérin, Winifred. *Charlotte Brontë*. Oxford: Clarendon Press, 1967.

Gérin, Winifred. *Emily Brontë*. Oxford: Clarendon Press, 1971.

Glen, Heater, ed. *The Cambridge Companion to the Brontës*. New York: Cambridge University Press, 2002.

Gordon, Lyndall. *Charlotte Brontë: A Passionate Life*. New York: W. W. Norton and Company, 1994.

"Jane Eyre." (2013). Wikipedia.
http://en.wikipedia.org/wiki/Jane_Eyre

Knapp, Bettina. *The Brontës*. New York:
Continuum, 1992.

Lane, Margaret. *The Brontë Story*. Westport, CT:
Greenwood Press, 1953.

Miller, Lucasta. *The Brontë Myth*. New York:
Knopf, 2001.

"Patrick Brontë." (2013). Wikipedia.
**http://en.wikipedia.org/wiki/Patrick_Bront%C3%A
B**

Reef, Catherine. *The Brontë Sisters: The Brief
Lives of Charlotte, Emily, and Anne*. New York:
Houghton Mifflin, 2012. E-book.

"Shirley." (2013). Wikipedia.
http://en.wikipedia.org/wiki/Shirley_(novel)

"The Tenant of Wildfell Hall." (2013). Wikipedia.
**http://en.wikipedia.org/wiki/The_Tenant_of_Wildf
ell_Hall**

"Villette." (2013). Wikipedia.
http://en.wikipedia.org/wiki/Villette_(novel)

Vine, Stephen. *Emily Brontë*. New York: Twayne Publishers, 1998.

"Wuthering Heights." (2013). Wikipedia.
http://en.wikipedia.org/wiki/Wuthering_Heights

Manufactured by Amazon.ca
Bolton, ON